FREE TV.

THE COMPLETE GUIDE TO DITCHING CABLE & SAVING $1000s WITHOUT SACRIFICING YOUR SHOWS

J. J. Streetman

Copyright © 2015 by Bright Ideas Editoria Ltd.

First Printing: 2015
Bright Ideas Editorial
PO Box 4095
Crested Butte, CO 81224
http://www.brightideaseditoria.com

Facts at Your Fingertips

Disclaimer

Although the author and publisher have made every effort to ensure that the information in this book was correct at press time, the author and publisher do not assume and hereby disclaim any liability to any party for any loss, damage, or disruption caused by errors or omissions, whether such errors or omissions result from negligence, accident, or any other cause.

Neither the author or publisher have any relationship with any of the products, networks, programs or websites in this book, except where explicitly mentioned, and have no control over the content. The information is presented solely as a service. The author and publisher do not assume and hereby disclaim any responsibility for any loss, damage, or disruption that happens while using any of the products, applications, or websites in this book. Not all of the information is this book can be applied everywhere. Check with your laws to make sure that you are compliant.

As a thank you for purchasing this book, I've created a special report to show you the most popular shows you can watch for free without a subscription. I can't include this inside the book and still keep it up to date, so click on the link below to receive the most up to date version.

GET THE FREE LIST NETFLIX™ AND HULU™ DON'T WANT YOU TO SEE!!!

138 Popular TV Shows You Can Watch For FREE Anytime (No Subscription Required!)
http://editoria.leadpages.co/138shows

Table of Contents

Why I Wrote This Book

Two years ago, my family made the decision to move to the mountains for the winter so that our children could get their fill of the ski slopes. We made another decision at the same time: we would get rid of our cable bill.

Our decision was primarily a financial one. We looked at the $100 + we were sending to our cable company every month and figured that that $1200 per year would be better spent on a vacation. We psyched ourselves up for all of the productive ways we would spend our time without television. We needn't have bothered. The reality is that we watch far more television now than ever before.

When we got rid of cable, in essence, the only things we eliminated were restrictions. We used to ask, "What is on?" Our choices were limited to what we had recorded on the DVR, the movies we'd bought, and, of course, current programming. Now we ask, "What do we want to watch?" And then we figure out how to watch it. It is fantastically liberating. And completely portable, whether we are staying at a hotel or in Central America. But it does come with some frustration.

The first issue we ran into was football season. The Sunday night game is the only one that is streamed live online, and you can't buy an online football subscription without a cable one, in the US. Many of the sites that stream sports on the internet are scary and download viruses to your computer. But we figured it out, and I give you the solution in the chapter called "Sports".

Another issue was HBO programming, because, at the time, HBO didn't sell an online only subscription. They now do, so it is no longer an issue, but I share the solution we used under "Hacks" and you won't believe it.

And then you'll be hooked.

Transitioning from cable to internet based television required a change in our mindset. This broadening of our vision has encouraged us as a family to redefine how we look at so many established traditions. Why do we do this in that way? Is there a better way for us to do it? And the more we ask and answer that question, the closer our lives get what we consider ideal.

As with anything new, it takes some adjustment. There were times when we were really annoyed that everything didn't work like it used to. But looking back, I'm so happy we made the switch. We now have a much richer relationship with not just television, but technology in general.

Happy cord cutting!

Why You Should Read This Book

Cord cutting is the next evolution of television, and it is happening right now. First there was radio. Then came black and white TV. Then color. But there were only three big networks plus a few local stations. Then cable networks began popping up, first a few, and then hundreds. Then came DVRs so people could record what they wanted from nearly a thousand channels of programming. And yet, at times, there is still *nothing on.*

Ten years from now, television will be a different experience from what it is today. People will still watch programming on TVs of increasingly larger size, but they will also watch it on their computers, tablets, and smartphones. In fact, many tech savvy folks do so already.

If the idea of cable companies going away, or evolving into something new, scares you, I get it. Status Quo is comfortable, and change is very uncomfortable. And this is a huge change, much harder to wrap your arms around than just switching from black-and-white to color. But the rewards for accepting and embracing the change are two-fold:

The first is financial. While you won't completely eliminate the funds you pay toward home entertainment each month, you will hopefully reduce it, and better control what content you receive for the amount that you pay. My family saves over $1000 per year, and we only had basic services on our cable bill.

The second is control. When you give up cable and opt for receiving your home entertainment through the internet, you have unprecedented access to a variety of content. You are in the driver's seat, not the cable company. You will always be able to find quality content, and not be at the mercy of what providers feel like delivering at the moment.

A few years ago, Netflix, which started as a mail-order DVD rental service and has morphed into one of the largest providers of streaming content, began producing their own television series, and releasing the episodes all at once. This was a huge because it acknowledged that the way people watch TV has changed. People now prefer to 'binge-watch' a whole season over a weekend instead of patiently waiting for the next episode each week.

HBO recently changed their policy of requiring internet subscribers to first have a cable subscription, another nod to the TV watching evolution.

Most cable companies initially tried to ignore the trend. They were used to subscribers being dependent on them, used to charging increasingly higher rates for content they had a monopoly over. Those that do not change will eventually go away. Look at Blockbuster. Fifteen years ago, Blockbuster was the biggest movie rental chain, and now they are gone because they didn't acknowledge that people were looking for a different experience than what they offered. Cable companies that don't understand that consumers are looking for ala carte programming instead of package deals will die as well.

Some cable and satellite providers are now paying attention, though they are stuck in the same mindset. DISH Network recently spun off Sling TV, which mimics a cable subscription on a streaming device or computer, with, albeit, a more limited number of channels, but some important ones like ESPN. Direct TV has also responded in a limited way by allowing customers to stream movies over their boxes, bringing some of the features cord cutters are looking for to their model. Other cable companies are going a different route, offering expanded services to the small screen for a staggeringly inflated monthly charge. It will be interesting to see how these companies continue to evolve with the new paradigm.

The world of cord-cutting really is a modern day wild west. There is no standard model yet; there are no established practices; providers are just making it up as they go and adapting to consumer response. For consumers, the laws are murky and unenforced; cord cutters ask only "how can I do this" and not "is this allowed?" Content creators are being forced to come up with new ways to earn money now that distribution is a free-for-all.

As a consumer, you have a lot of big choices. Will you add a streaming device to your entertainment system? Which one do you pick? Will it meet all of your needs, or will you keep your cable provider too? Some choices can lead to a more complicated system, and some can lead to paying out an even higher amount every month.

This book sets out the basics of transitioning your TV experience from cable to the internet. It walks you through the hardware (streaming devices) and software (apps) that you need and shows you how to look for and take advantage of trends as they change. It shows you how to immerse yourself in the pool slowly instead of pushing you off the diving board into the deep end right away. It also shows you all of the tips and tricks of advanced users so that when you get to the deep end, you'll be the one doing flips off the side, not the one facing the wrong end of a super soaker squirt gun.

I guarantee you that making the change will cause you some frustration. It will irritate you at times. But in a year, I also promise that you will wonder why your friends still have a cable box or ugly satellite dish on the side of their home. You will be a more content and knowledgeable consumer, with all of the bragging rights that entails. And if you don't like it, you'll be in the driver's seat when it comes to renegotiating terms with your cable company. In fact, many companies are offering huge incentives to get cord cutters back. It is a win-win either way.

Ready to get started? The first chapter gives you an overview of life without cable.

Chapter One: What do You Need to Watch TV Without Cable or Satellite?

Cord cutters throw around a lot of terms: HULU™, Netflix™, Roku™, Apple TV™, Fire TV™, streaming, bandwidth, Gbps. It can feel like a foreign language. What are all of these things, and how do they work?

Most of the terms you hear batted about by cord cutters refer to the specific names of devices or applications. We will cover specific products in later chapters. For now, we are going to cover, in general, the basics that you need to know about to become a cord cutter. The first thing we need to understand is what it means to stream something from the internet.

What Is the Difference Between Streaming and Downloading?

There are two different ways to access movies and television shows from the internet. You can download them, or you can stream them. Each method has its pros and cons.

Downloading is the traditional way that people have accessed content from the internet. When you download a file, you transfer a copy of that file to the long-term storage on your device. You are then able to access that content whenever you like. DVRs that you use to record cable shows work this way. They store the content until you delete it from the storage device. iTunes™ also works this way. When you buy a song, you then download it to your Mp3 player and can listen to it as often as you like. (You can also download movies and TV shows from iTunes, but we'll get to that later). The benefits of this method are that once you download the content it is readily available, even if you don't have an internet connection handy. Many people download movies to their computers or tablets to watch on airplane flights. The disadvantage to downloading is that it fills up your storage, and you need to actively manage your hard drive, deleting old files when you no longer want them. Sometimes it can be rough just remembering where you have stored content on your device if your device doesn't manage that part for you.

When you stream content, it is delivered in real-time to your device. You are still downloading the data, but your device deletes it once you watch it, so you don't have to actively manage it. YouTube™ works this way. The advantage of this method is that the content becomes disposable; you watch it and it disappears. It also often costs less to stream than to download. I think of it like the difference between renting and buying video tapes, or like borrowing a book from the library instead of purchasing it from a book store. The disadvantage to streaming is that you need to have an internet connection to access streamed content. Also, sometimes the content is no longer available when you want to watch it again later, or you can't find where you watched it. Most of the television and movie content that is watched by cord cutters is streamed.

What are the Basics that you Need to Watch Television over the Internet?

To watch television over the internet, you need three things in addition to your TV: a high-speed internet connection, a device to stream the programs, and applications that provide the content. That is it. The rest of this book is dedicated to the various options and nuances of those three things.

A high-speed internet connection is the most critical of the three. Without a high-speed connection, your experience will all about waiting and interruptions. It will be like your television suddenly turned into a two-year-old with all of the tantrums and mess that implies. The next chapter defines what a high-speed connection is, shows you how to test your connection, and gives you some tips on increasing your speed.

A streaming device is a piece of hardware that connects your television to the internet. This will replace your cable box and DVR. It can be a regular old laptop, or a specific product sold for that purpose, like a Roku box or a Fire Stick. The type of device you use determines how robust your television and movie experience will be. Chapter Three on streaming devices covers the advantages and disadvantages of the different kinds of devices so that you can choose what will work best for you and your family.

Applications are like television and movie channels that provide that actual content. Applications are the key to finding the content you want to watch. Apps can be specific to the device you are using, and different devices have access to different apps. Apps, however, are not the only way to find content, and many shows are also streamed from websites on the internet. Chapter four covers the most popular apps and also shows you other places to find content.

Once you understand the basics and get up and running, you'll realize that not all content is available from the apps and internet sites that you have access to, and that can be crushing. NFL and college football are prime examples. Chapter five, sports, shows you ways to stream popular sporting events over the internet without downloading dangerous viruses to your computer.

Once you see how, with a little effort, you can stream most sporting events, you'll realize that you have access to most programming from all over the world. Want to watch *Downton Abbey* when it first shows in England instead of waiting three months for PBS to air it? Want to access American Netflix options from Australia? Want to eliminate many commercials? Chapter Six, Hacks, shows you the advanced tricks experienced cord cutters use to ramp their online viewing up to eleven.

The world of streaming online content changes rapidly. As soon as you get comfortable, something new comes along to shake it all up. Chapter Seven is a list of resources for you to use: places to turn to when you have questions, blogs that keep up with changes, etc.

One note of caution: Before cancelling your cable subscription, read the fine print on your contract. Many users find out the hard way that even though they have been customers of their cable provider for years and aren't locked into a contract, the cable company requires a number of months of advance warning before you break up, sort of a cable prenup. They might insist you continue to pay a bill for an additional 1-6 months!

Moving from cable or satellite is exciting, scary, rewarding, and confusing. Take it step by step. If you run into problems, send a message to my Facebook page called Lose Your Cable, and we'll try to help you out.

Chapter Two: High-Speed Internet Access

The term High-Speed Internet Access is a generic term that doesn't have a precise definition. Internet providers use it to describe anything faster than dial-up access, which isn't helpful.

The quick and dirty solution is to pay for the fastest internet offered in your area. It will be worth it to you as you become a heavier internet user, and it will pay for itself when you get rid of your cable bill. The FCC in the US recommends purchasing a service that offers speeds of 15 Mbps or better if you're going to be doing lots of streaming[1]. For some readers, that might be all the information you want about high-speed internet access. If so, feel free to skip to the next chapter. Other readers might be interested in learning what 15 Mbps means, how to test your actual internet speed, how broadband differs from internet speed, and how to make sure the internet is as fast as possible in your household. If so, read on.

How is Internet Speed Measured?

Internet speed is measured in units of bits per second. A bit is the smallest unit of data used by a computer. Just as a letter is the smallest unit into which you divide a word, a bit cannot be subdivided. Bits can only have two values, 0 and 1. In measuring how fast the 0s and 1s are flying from where they are stored on the internet to your device, you will see the following abbreviations:

Unit	Definition	Bits per second
bps or bit/s	Bits per second	1
Bps	Bytes per second – a byte is 8 bits	8
Kbps or Kbit/s	Kilobits per second – a kilobit is 1024 bits*	1024
KBps	Kilobytes per second – a kilobyte is 1024 bytes	8192

Mbps or Mbit/s	Megabits per second – a megabit is 1024 kilobits	1,048,576
MBps	Megabytes per second – a megabyte is 1024 kilobytes	8,388,608
Gbps or Gbit/s	Gigabits per second – a gigabit is 1024 megabits	1,073,741,824
GBps	Gigabytes per second – a gigabyte is 1024 megabytes	8,589,934,592

*You often see kilobits approximated to 1000 bits, megabits approximated to 1000 kilobits, etc. because round numbers are easier to work with.

Easy enough right? Where this can get confusing is that speed is almost always talked about in terms of bits per second while files are usually measured in bytes. So if the file you wanted to download is 1 MB (1 megabyte), and your connection speed is 1 Mbps, it will take roughly 8 seconds to download that file, not one second.

How Fast is Fast Enough?

The answer to how fast is fast enough, is, of course, it depends. In this case, it depends on how highly defined you want the picture to be.

If you have an HD television and enjoy that crisp HD picture, you are going to need a connection speed that is two to three times faster than if you don't care about HD. It takes lots more bits of data to produce that high definition.

If you consider that an average non-HD 45-minute television show is 200 MB, then to stream the show without interruption, in theory, you would need a connection speed fast enough to deliver the show in 45 minutes. Forty-five minutes is 2700 seconds. 200 MB is 1638400 bits (200 x 8 x 1024). That works out to needing a connection speed at least 607 bps. The same show in HD is 600 MBs, so you would need a theoretical connection speed of 1821 bps (1.77 kbps) just for that program.

In reality, though, it takes longer to stream a show than the pure numbers we calculated above for various reasons. There is other data that your device is exchanging with the internet. It is updating catalogs of shows, providing information about where you are located, so the data streams to the right place, etc.

Consider also that it is unlikely that your streaming device will enjoy the entire bandwidth provided by your internet service provider all to itself.

What is the Difference Between Bandwidth and Internet Speed?

Bandwidth and internet speed are often used interchangeably, but they don't mean the same thing.

Bandwidth is the maximum internet speed that your internet service provider (ISP) promises you between their connection point and your router. The name 'bandwidth' implies that it is measuring area instead of speed because bandwidth is the size of the 'internet pipeline' your ISP has allocated to just you.

For the majority of homes today, the internet comes in via cable or fiber optics from your ISP to a router. The router then shares the internet throughout the home via a wireless network. Most people have many devices that are connected to the internet via their router: devices like smartphones, televisions, computers, laptops, tablets, gaming devices, etc. Every device that is connected to your router is sharing the same broadband. The more devices that are currently uploading and downloading content to and from the internet, the slower your actual connection speed will be. So if you spouse is chatting with his brother via FaceTime™ or Skype™ and your ten-year-old is playing on a Minecraft™ server, you are going to get a much slower internet speed than you would if you sent them both out of the house to do the grocery shopping. Even if the devices that are connected aren't being used actively, the programs on those devices could still be uploading or downloading information that they need to run smoothly.

It is an imperfect analogy, but I compare it to a hot water heater. We have a 30-gallon hot water heater, which means there is usually enough hot water for me to take a splendid bath in my spa tub, read a book, drink a cup of tea, and meditate without the water turning cold. But if both my kids jump in the shower at the same time and my husband starts a load of dishes, I'll run out of hot before the water level covers my ankles.

I've also seen broadband compared to a freeway. You have a maximum speed limit which is the broadband number your ISP brags about. You have multiple lanes on the freeway, which means multiple drivers can be on the road going the speed limit at the same time. But when you get too many cars, the actual speed of traffic invariably slows down below the speed limit, sometimes to just a crawl during rush hour.

So while you might be paying for broadband speed of up to 2 Mbps, in theory, you could still run into a buffering problem where the stream takes longer to load than to watch, even though the show only requires a speed of less than 2 Kbps to download. In reality, your actual speed can be more than 1000 times slower than your ideal broadband speed.

Another reason for the speed slowdown has to do with how fast the data travels from your router to your device. Broadband speeds only cover the distance from your ISP's door to yours. Your router might be old, or slow. The closer you are to the access point, the faster the data will travel. The settings on your devices can make a difference as well. The Section of Ways to Increase Internet Speed goes through these in detail.

How to Test Your Actual Speed?

Lots of sites on the internet will test your speed for you. I like the one at www.speedtest.net. Note that it is normal for your upload speed (the rate at which you upload things like pictures to Facebook) to be much slower than your download speed. Just click on the link from a device you want to test.

Ways to Increase Internet Speed

If you are paying for filet mignon but receiving a hamburger, there are a lot of things you can do to increase your speed.

1. Replace your old router. Look on your router for the set of numbers 802.11 followed by a letter. If that letter comes before the letter n, it is time to replace it. What does the number mean? The body that codifies standards for internet technology is called the IEEE (Institute of Electrical and Electronic Engineers) and 802.11 is the protocol number that refers to wireless networking standards. Each new update of the standard is designated by the letter that comes at the end. The original

standard was 802.11, the first update was 802.11a, the next was 802.11b, all the way through z, and starting over with aa, then ab, and so on. 802.11n came about in 2009 and increases network speed by using a wider frequency channel and multiple input-output (MIMO) technology.

You might still need to replace an old 802.11n router if it has worn out. Heat can damage and slow down a router.

Rick Brioda from PC World suggests buying a new router at a store that offers a 30-day money back guarantee.[2] If it increases your speed, keep it. If not, return it and continue troubleshooting.

2.   Move the router closer to the computer or connect it with an Ethernet cable. Think of Wi-Fi like having a conversation. If the person is close to you, your messages will travel back and forth no problem, like when everyone is sitting at the dinner table. But if you are yelling

upstairs for your son to wash his hands (with soap this time) and come to dinner but his door is closed, and he is playing loud music, you may have to shout several times, depending on how loud your voice is and how worried he is that you might just toss his cell phone down the garbage disposal once and for all. But if you had an intercom that went right into his room, and it silenced his music at the same time, well, he'd hear you right away. Ethernet is a little like this, and for that reason it is often faster than Wi-Fi. Of course, if the router is in the basement, you may have to get a very long Ethernet cable and staple it behind picture frames, or hire an electrician to do it nicely. Alternatively, you might be able to move the router. Sometimes, there is more than one network jack in the house that you can plug it into.

3.   Purchase a wireless range extender or expander. This acts likes a repeater and boosts your signal strength between the router and the

device if you can't move them closer or connect them with an Ethernet cable. Look for extenders that just plug into an outlet and do not need to be configured.

4.   Upgrade the antenna on your router (remember sticking tinfoil balls on your car antennae?).

5.   Make sure your firmware is up to date. All devices, such as your router, your smartphone, your computer, and your streaming device, use software to manage that device's activities. That software is called firmware. Companies update their firmware all the time to handle new technology or fix old bugs. Your device should automatically update the new firmware as it is released, but errors can happen. To check if you need to update the firmware on your device, visit the website for that product. You can type "update firmware for" whatever make and model you need to check right into Google, and you should find many helpful links.

6. Check the link rate on your device. If some devices, like your phone, seem to stream faster than say, your old computer, it might be your computer itself that is the limiting factor. The app on or the operating system might not be processing the data at the rate it is receiving the data. Think of Lucy in the chocolate factory. She just couldn't keep up with the conveyor belt. It could be time to upgrade your old laptop.

7. Time of day matters. You are going to get a slower rate during peak traffic times, like in the evening. Not much you can do except make sure everything else is maximized.

8. Change the frequency on your router from 5 GHz (which optimizes speed) to 2.4 GHz (which optimizes range). Remember back when AM stations were popular, and on some nights you used to be able to pick up stations from other states? The lower frequency, longer wavelength waves travel further than their higher frequency counterparts. To change the

frequency on your router, you can't do it by flipping a switch on the device; instead you need to log on to the user interface of the device. See the section on connecting to your router to log on to it, and then adjust the frequency.

9.   Make sure your router is password protected. If it isn't, your neighbors could be stealing your bandwidth. True story: I once rented a house for a short-term in a different city. It was in the lease that I had to pay for all utilities including the internet. The connection speed seemed slow to me, so the first thing I did was to change the password on the router via the user interface (see Connecting to Your Router). I got a call from the property manager the next day asking if my internet was working OK because she had received a complaint from the neighbor that it was down. He was stealing my internet, and had the nerve to call and grouse about not being able to do it anymore!

Password protecting your router is more than a matter of protecting your bandwidth. It is a matter of protecting your data. Years ago, a friend of mine posted her outgoing bills in her mailbox, and they were stolen by a thief. The person ordered checks with her checking account number on them and cleaned out her account. When you access your banking data over an unsecured internet connection, you are leaving yourself similarly vulnerable. A clever thief could intercept your account information, and use it.

10. Change the channel. If you live in an apartment building or in another dense area, your speed might be slow because you might be getting interference from all your neighbors. Many routers use the same default settings. Have you ever used walkie talkies and picked up someone else's conversation on the same channel? It is the same principle with routers. You can download free tools to see what channel the neighbors are using

http://www.nirsoft.net/utils/wifi_informatio n_view.html. Then you can select a different channel using your router's user interface. See connecting to your Router below.

Connecting to Your Router

To connect to the user interface of your router, you need three things: the IP address of the device, the user name, and the password. Note that the interface user name and password are different from the device name and password that you use to connect to the router.

Keep in mind that even if your internet speed seems to be fine right now, there will come a day when you need to make friends with your router. I recommend that you figure out the user interface for it sooner rather than later if you have not already. If there comes a day when you need to access it, knowing what you are doing will keep your blood pressure in check.

Finding the IP address.

To find the IP address of your router, you can open up a "command prompt" on a Windows computer connected to the router, or the "terminal" if the connected machine is a Mac. Don't let this step scare you. You won't break anything. Unfortunately, the command prompt is located in different places on different Windows operating systems. For instance, using Windows 8, you just need to swipe from the right side of the screen and type "cmd prompt" into the search box. On Windows 7, you hit the Start Button, then All Programs, then Accessories, then Command Prompt. If you can't find it, don't get frustrated. Google the search term "cmd prompt" and the operating system you are using. There is sure to be a YouTube tutorial for how to find it.

Once you have a command prompt window open, you will see a blinking curser. Don't worry about anything else you see. For a windows machine, type the word "ipconfig" (without the quotes) at the blinking curser. Look on YouTube for a tutorial if you want extra help.

From a Mac, you type "ifconfig –a" (the cursor won't be blinking). Look for tutorials on YouTube.

Scroll down the page looking for the words "Default Gateway". It will look something like:

Default Gateway . . . .:192.168.1.1

Make a note of the numbers. Write them down.

Now, open up a browser window, like Google Chrome or IE Explorer. Clear out anything that might be in the address bar, that line at the top of the screen where you would normally type a web address, like www.Amazon.com. Type just the number into the address bar. In this case, I would type 192.168.1.1 into the address bar.

If you did it correctly, a login window will appear. If you don't know the user name and password, I have a number of steps for you to try.

- Call the person who helped set up your network to see if they know

- Try using 'admin' (without the quotes) for the user name. If that doesn't work, try 'administrator' (without the quotes).

- The most common passwords are admin, administrator, password, and nothing (leave it blank).

- If all of those fail, you can look on the router for clues, and look in the documentation that came with the router.

- The last resort would be to reset the router with the reset button on the router itself. This will reset the security, password, etc. on the router, so be careful doing it. This will reset the user name and password as well, so you can change it to something memorable. You will probably need to reconnect all your devices when you are done.

Once you are logged in to your router, what you see might be confusing. Spend some time looking around, trying to get a sense of which tab does what. If you can't find what you are looking for after a while, don't get frustrated. Try googling the search term for what you are trying to do along with the name of your router. For example, google "How to change channel on a Netgear router". Read through the results that come up until you find one that walks you through it, preferably with pictures.

As a side note, if your Wi-Fi password is the default annoying string of letters and numbers, here is where you can change it to something more memorable. Have you seen the internet cartoons (memes) that say: "Dear children, want today's password? Make your bed, empty the dishwasher, and it's yours!"

You can also change the name of the router to something more easy to find, like "Jen's Router" instead Neatgear12345.

Lastly, if your user name and password on the router are the defaults, change then to something more secure, so your neighbors can't hack you so easily.

Once you are satisfied that you have an internet connection that is fast enough and reliable enough to stream television and movies, your next step is to select the streaming device that fits your needs. The next section covers the various types of streaming devices and their pros and cons to help you make an informed decision.

Chapter Three: Streaming Devices

A streaming device is a piece of hardware that connects your television to the internet. With some newer smart TVs, the technology is actually already imbedded in the TV itself, and you may decide you don't need an external device.

What's confusing about streaming devices is that they don't all have access to the same set of applications. Think of the apps as different channels. So before you can select a device, you need to have a rough idea of what programming you are going to want access to, and make sure your device can support it.

Another criterion to consider is how easy the device is to use. If your sanity is tied to your three-year-old being able to watch *Dinosaur Train* on weekend mornings without waking you, then you need a device that she can navigate by pushing buttons and recognizing pictures. If, on the other hand, you consider yourself a tech whiz and want maximum content, you'll want a set up that is more responsive.

Cost too is a consideration. Streaming devices can cost under $40 or more than $400. I was lucky enough to get my first device for free from an uncle who decided he couldn't be bothered with it. You might be able to find a used slightly older model for a bargain on sites like Craigslist, eBay, Nextdoor, etc.

Extra considerations some users have are the gaming capabilities of the device, whether your current digital library is platform specific, whether a new device will work with their surround sound setup, and other technical specifications.

Finally, most cord cutters get an HD or OTA antenna to complement their streaming device. It is the digital equivalent of the old rabbit ears antennas that allow you to watch local commercial channels live for free (with reception equal to cable or internet). This is especially handy for people who like to watch local news and local sports in real time.

My quick and dirty recommendation is that if you just want to dip your toe in the pool to see how warm the water is, get a Roku 3 player, and use it for several months in conjunction with your current cable set up. Right now, Roku has the most apps, and it is the easiest device to search for content. If you want to jump straight into the shark-infested ocean without a divers cage, connect a laptop running Windows 8 or higher to your set with an HDMI cord and skip a specialty device altogether. If this answered your questions, feel free to move to the next chapter about apps to run on your device. If, on the other hand, you want more information about the various devices so you can make up your own mind, read on!

Types of Streaming Devices

Streaming devices come in many forms, so it might not be obvious at first glance that they all have the same purpose. There are boxes that connect to the TV via an HDMI cable, tiny sticks that plug into an HDMI port on the TV, gaming consoles that also have some streaming channels, televisions that connect to the internet, and laptops. As outlined above, the basic things you'll want to know about are apps, ease of use, cost, and the exciting special features of the device to compare them and make a decision. The chart below is a light weight comparison of the most popular streaming devices. It breaks down the high level criteria by manufacturer and device type to you can see what you need to know (I'm not getting paid in any way to endorse any of them):

Amazon Fire TV

Cost: About $99

Apps: Catching up to Roku quickly with over 1500 apps and games. It has all of the major ones like Netflix, Amazon Instant Video, Sling TV, Showtime, and Pandora, and they just added HBO NOW. The big exception is no access to iTunes content. The full channel line-up can be found at: http://www.amazon.com/b/ref=sv_mas_4?ie=UTF8&node=703143301.

Pros – Very easy to use. You access channels with a remote control that also responds to your voice for many commands, including search functions. The remote uses radio frequencies to communicate with the device, so you can point the remote anywhere, and it should work. It doesn't have to have line-of-site with the device. It has more games available than Roku. If you have an Amazon phone or tablet, the devices integrate well, and you can 'fling' what is on your phone or tablet to the television and use the handheld device as a remote. This expands the content you can view. You can also use Bluetooth headphones with it so you won't wake the kids. The Fire TV gives added features, such as access to the IMDB database, to shows you watch on Amazon Instant Video that you don't get when you watch the channel on other devices.

Cons – Some users are annoyed that it prioritizes Amazon content over other apps. Also, it doesn't have the ability to search across multiple channels for content, so searching can be tedious.

Amazon Fire TV Stick

Cost: About $39

Apps: Same as Fire TV

Pros: This device is tiny and plugs into an HDMI port on your TV, a big plus for wall mounted televisions. You can also use Amazon tablets and phones with it to 'fling' content and expand your viewing selection, and you get the extra Amazon Instant Video features.

Cons: Like the Fire TV, it prioritizes Amazon content over content from other channels. It doesn't have voice search, and can't connect Bluetooth headphones.

Amazon Fire TV Gamers Bundle

Cost: About $144

Apps: Same as Fire TV

Pros: This is a Fire TV with a gaming control console and extra cable, so it has all the features of a Fire TV and more. The Fire TV has a faster processor than Roku, which matters more for gaming that watching flicks.

Cons: Same as Fire TV. Also, it is more of a lighter gaming experience than what you would get with an Xbox or Sony device.

Apple TV

Cost: About $69

Apps: Apple TV has only a fraction of channels compared to Amazon Fire or Roku, and no games. They still have many of the major apps like Netflix, HULU, and HBO Now with the notable exceptions of Pandora and Amazon Instant Video (you can share these to the TV from another i-device, though). See the channel lineup at http://www.apple.com/shop/buy-appletv/appletv.

Pros: If you also have an iPad, iTouch, or iPhone, you can use the AirPlay™ feature to project a wider variety of content to the screen – basically anything you can access through a browser, even if Apple TV doesn't have an app for it. In this way, it combines both easy and more sophisticated usage. Apple TV is a fan favorite among people who use i-devices heavily. Uses can watch any of the movies and TV shows that they have bought on iTunes and share among other devices and family members. Because these can be downloaded to devices, you can watch them away from an internet connection on iPads, etc.

Cons: Users complain that the Apple TV is slightly harder than other devices because it doesn't have voice search, and new channels appear on the menu whether you have a subscription or not. A big drawback is that Apple TV doesn't have any games. You can play games on smaller devices and project them to the bigger screen, but since you still have to stare at the smaller screen to play the game, it has limited value.

Note that Apple is rolling out a bigger, badder version in Fall 2015 that will have voice search, games, and so much more, so you will hold off if you're an Apple fan, and see if the new device is a game changer.

Chromecast

About $35

Apps: It has access to most of the popular apps like Netflix and HULU, with a few very big holes. You can't get Amazon Instant Video or Sling TV app directly, but you can use the casting feature to cast those from the small screen to the big screen. It is the only device with a Google Play app. HBO NOW is set to roll out on Chromecast soon. Look at http://www.google.com/chrome/devices/chromecast/apps.html for the complete channel selection.

Pros: This is a small stick that plugs right into an HDMI port, so it is great with wall mounted sets. You can cast to the screen with the widest variety of devices, pretty much any laptop, any Android tablet or phone, and I believe Apple devices now as well. It is the least expensive streaming device. It is popular with users who have purchased lots of movies, TV shows, games and music on Google Play.

Cons: Chromecast doesn't come with its own remote. You need to control it with a smartphone or tablet, so this option is tough for kids who can't type in passwords or users who are intimidated by technology. The nice part is you can use an Apple, Windows or Android device to control it. There are some complaints that the mirroring function from the small screen to the big one doesn't work well. There is no voice search or ability to search across different channels.

Nexus Player
Cost: About $70

Apps: The big ones, like Netflix and Hulu Plus, and lots of games. As of this writing, I was unable to find a complete list. Channels and games are added via the Google Play store.

Pros: Built by ASUS, this is an Android device that that is designed to integrate with Google Play movies, etc. The voice search function uses Google, so it is best in class, and provides results from multiple apps at once. You can cast to it from a variety of Windows, Apple, or Chromebook devices, and the content is supposed to synch across Android devices. You can add a gaming console to enhance gaming.

Cons: Not as many apps available yet, and they can be hard to find though the list is constantly growing. It is a newer device, so not as thoroughly reviewed as others so far.

Roku 1

Cost: About $49

Apps: The largest selection of channels, 2000 + Including Netflix, Hulu, Amazon Instant Video, Showtime, PBS, History Channel, CBS, Comedy Central, Pandora, etc. No access to iTunes or Google Play, and no agreement with HBO NOW yet (but you can get HBO through Sling TV). See the full selection at https://www.roku.com/channels#!browse/new.

Pros: This is one of the few devices that will work with older televisions that don't have HDMI ports. Use the Roku remote to scroll through channels and shows. You can type in a search across many channels, which is extremely handy.

Cons: No voice search. No built in functionality to project the small screen to the large one.

Roku 2

Cost: About $59

Apps: Same as Roku 1

Pros: Easy to use and faster than Roku 1. You can search across many channels at once, which is really handy, and it doesn't prioritize content from one source over another. When you are looking for a specific TV show or movie, you can check Netflix,

Amazon Instant Video, HULU PLUS, Crackle and others all at once (assuming you subscribe to them). You can even search by actor. You can also mirror your Windows or Android smartphone, tablet or PC to a 2015 Roku 2, which greatly expands your selection.

Cons: No voice search.

Roku 3

Cost: About $99

Apps: Same as Roku 1 and 2

Pros: All of the pros of a Roku 2, such as mirroring, and searching across multiple channels. This top of the line model also includes voice search, similar to Siri or OK Google, so when you yell at the TV, it listens to you. The Roku 3 also has a 'Point Anywhere' remote that uses radio frequencies, so you don't have to have a line of site with the box. The remote has motion control for some games, in the tradition of a Wii, and a wired headphone jack so you can read a book while your spouse watches a show. The wired headphone jack is easier to use for kids than a wireless one and works with any headphones. This is my pick for the best all-around device.

Roku Streaming Stick
About $49

Same as Roku 1, 2, & 3

Pros: It has the mirroring and searching across multiple channels like Roku 2 & 3, and the 'Point Anywhere' remote. It plugs directly into an HDMI slot, so it is good for wall mounted sets.

Cons: No voice search, headphone jack, or motion controller for games in the remote.

Xbox 360
Price: About $250

Apps: The 'largest selection of games', thousands, and serious gaming capability. Xbox 360 has access to all of the major television apps like Amazon Instant Video, Netflix, HULU PLUS, etc., with an emphasis on sports channels. They also have a special relationship with ESPN with a lot of features, but you need a cable subscription to access everything. Go to http://www.xbox.com/en-US/entertainment/xbox-360/live-apps for a full list of channels.

Pros: Because this was a gaming device first and a streaming device second, it has functionality that the other devices haven't thought of, like split screen action. If you have a Kinect sensor, you can use some voice commands and gestures to control and search on the device. The 'PlayTo' function lets you beam content from small devices to the big one. In countries outside of the US, users can beam the TV to their smartphone or tablet (in addition to the other way around).

Cons: To take advantage of the WatchESPN functionality, you still need a cable subscription or Sling TV subscription and an internet provider that pays ESPN extra. Some consumers have had problems with the device overheating.

Xbox One

Price: About $349

Apps: Its game library is catching up to the 360, and the newest games are being released for this model first. Like the 360, it has access to the major television apps with an emphasis on sports.

Pros: This is the newest, biggest, baddest gaming device from Microsoft, and it is much more powerful that the 360. It is also larger than the Xbox 360 and because of that it is supposed to be more stable and is not supposed to overheat. Like the 360, this device it was designed first for gaming, and is a great way to watch sports, but you still need a cable or Sling TV subscription to make the most of it.

Cons: Higher cost.

Laptop running Windows 8 or higher

Price: Varies

Apps: Content is limitless. You can download most of the same channels as the other devices, or access the content directly from the networks website. This is the only way I know of to access iTunes, Google Play, Amazon Instant Video, Netflix, and HBO Now all in one place, plus thousands of other choices.

Pros: Endless content, and the ability to use lots of the hacks found in Chapter 6, like limiting commercials.

Cons: This system is less intuitive than using a specific device or smart TV, and the cost is greater if you are buying a new device for this purpose. Kids or older users could run into some trouble with this method.

Smart TV

Price: Varies

Apps: Many smart TVs have both built in apps like YouTube and Netflix, but they also have the ability to let you cast to it from a smaller device, like an iPad, laptop, or smartphone.

Pros: You can get both an intuitive experience where kids can power on the TV, select Netflix and search for a show, along with a more robust experience with the ability to cast to it from handheld devices.

Cons: An expensive way to go if you aren't in the market for a new TV. Many of the things you can do with a smart TV you can do with a dumb TV and an HDMI cord.

In addition to streaming devices that allow you to connect your TV to the internet, there are other devices out there designed for you to watch programs when you are away from the TV, and the tablets and phones you already have probably have lots of functionality as well. These devices don't connect directly to the big screen, although some work hand in hand with an additional streaming devices and allow you to either project your content to the screen or work as a second screen providing more information about what you are watching.

Before you make any final decisions, it is a good idea to check out all of the technical specification of the device. Will it work with your audio setup? How much memory does it have? How fast is the processor? What kind of Wi-Fi technology does it use? Will it work with your video library? What else can it do that you might care about later on?

It is also helpful to read current user reviews of the product. I find the best place to read reviews is on Amazon because of the sheer number of them (although it may or may not be the best place for you to ultimately buy the device). You will be able to see what people like about it and also problems you may not have thought of before. Most of the reviews are unbiased, though not always intelligible.

Before you purchase a device, do your homework. Shop for price both at brick and mortar stores and online. Look at the company's website for special deals, especially on older models. Look for warranties.

Finally, before you make a decision, read through the next chapter on content to get an idea of the types of apps that you will want. Make sure the device is compatible.

Chapter Four: Internet TV Channels

When I got my first Roku box, I think there were fewer than 20 channels. Now there are thousands. Some channels are free, some are free with commercials, some are available with a paid subscription, some have a paid subscription and still have commercials, and some are only available if you have a cable TV subscription. This last group thinks that users will continue to pay for cable content while using streaming devices to augment their cable experience. We've already seen this business model start to crumble, with HBO and Showtime recently offering online-only subscriptions, and CBS and NBC offering content free with commercials. It won't be long before the other big networks like ESPN follow. It will be interesting to see who waits too long and loses an unrecoverable percentage of market share before making the switch.

Because there are thousands of channels, the focus here is to provide information on two types of paid subscription channels: those that replicate content you are already watching on cable, and those that provide the biggest bang for the buck. But because the free channel selection is virtually endless, don't stop with these. Want Christian programming? There are hundreds of channels with free religious content. Like TED talks? There is a free TED TV channel. Many of the paid subscription channels give you a month for free to seed the hook. Also, look at individual network websites to see who streams for free in their own right. Some networks make you wait a week for the latest episode or show only a limited number of episodes, the last five for example. Some have great back content of old shows from over the decades.

My quick and dirty recommendation is to start with a subscription to both Amazon Prime and Netflix, and perhaps HULU PLUS as well depending on which networks you watch most, and then evaluate from there. But if you are looking for the nitty gritty on the most popular channels, read on! When browsing the apps available on specific devices, make sure to read the description to make sure a cable subscription is not required. And if you want to see where you can find a specific TV show or movie, check out www.moreflicks.com.

General Content Apps

Acorn TV - $4.99 per month. While you won't find Downton Abbey here (at least not yet), if you have a thing for British TV, especially vintage shows, this is a goldmine. Mysteries abound with lots of Agatha Christie, Inspector Morse, et al. My heart stopped when I saw the complete run of Lovejoy, Cadfael, I Claudius, Upstairs Downstairs, and lots more. Check out their lineup at https://acorn.tv/browse/browseall.

Amazon Prime - $99 per year. If you already use Amazon to regularly order anything, then a Prime membership is a no-brainer. With the subscription, you get free 2-day shipping on many of their products, free photo storage, lots of free music, and access to many free television shows and movies via Amazon Instant Video. Only a fraction of Amazon streamable content is free, though. Many more movies and TV shows are available to rent or purchase for a fee. I have found that Amazon and Netflix complement each other well because the same shows are rarely free on both channels.

Crackle – Free. Crackle has older movies, TV shows, and original content free with commercials. Even though the content is dated, many people still can find things they enjoy watching.

Google Play – No monthly fee to access movies and TV, but you have to pay to rent most of the content individually. Google Play has some free TV episodes (you still need to provide a credit card number), and a lot more for rent by episode or the entire season. They don't have any free movies unless it is a special promotion.

HULU PLUS- $8.99 - $11.99 per month. Many subscribers like HULU because it organizes content from over 100 different networks into one location. The drawback is that they add commercials. Up until now I have shunned HULU because the content I am personally interested in I can find free directly from the Networks' own websites, and I'm unwilling to pay a premium just to have it in one location. Also, HULU detects ad blockers and shows a blank screen instead of commercials, which is fair enough in this technological Wild West, but annoying all the same. Now, though, they have rolled out a commercial free subscription for a few dollars more each month. That makes for a more attractive product in my book. Definitely worth a look to see if they have the shows you want to watch.

iTunes – While there isn't a native iTunes app for most devices, if you have purchased content on iTunes, you can watch it on your TV by connecting or casting a tablet or computer to your big screen. iTunes is another place you can rent or buy TV shows and movies, much like Amazon Prime, YouTube, or Google Play.

Netflix – From $7.99 per month, depending on how many devices you have going at one time. Once you pay the monthly fee, all of the shows are included. We have the subscription for the maximum number of devices, and often my kids will each watch a separate show on their iPads while my husband and I are watching a show on the big screen. Netflix also produces its own quality content *like Orange is the New Black* and *House of Cards.* It is a good complement to an Amazon Prime Membership as there isn't much overlap.

Pandora – No subscription fees for music. Create your own personal stations based on a song, artist, or genre and listen free with commercials, or spend a few dollars a month to avoid them. You can't listen to specific songs (try YouTube for that), but you can customize the station to your tastes.

Sling TV - $20 for basic channels, lots of add-ons you can pay extra for. Sling TV is a child of DISH Network, and has a decidedly cable like feel to it. You pay for some basic channels, including ESPN, ESPN 2, HGTV, AMC, Food network, A&E, ABC Family, Lifetime, TBS, CNN, Bloomberg Television (you can find the complete lineup at https://www.sling.com/package). You have the option to add on packages like HBO, sports, Kids TV, world news. Right now it is available on most devices except Apple TV, and it is the only way I know of for cord cutters to legally get access to WatchESPN.

VEVO – No subscription fees for music videos.

Vimeo – Very similar to YouTube (see below). Content on Vimeo is uploaded by users who are usually the creators. You can find how-to content on pretty much anything, music videos, television programs and full-length movies.

VUDU – No subscription fees, this is a movie rental channel. Costs are similar to the other movie rental channels like Amazon Prime, Google Play, YouTube, and Apple TV.

YouTube – Most people use YouTube for the virtually endless free content, some of which is provided legitimately by the creator, and some of which is pirated. Many artists like it because it is a way to both gain exposure for their expertise and get paid for their work via ad revenue. It is all on there. (You can fast forward thorough many of the ads after a few seconds if you wish, or block them entirely with an ad blocker – see the section on hacks). Want to learn to knit, knead dough, practice yoga, play the violin, build a chicken coop, play Minecraft, remove viruses from your computer, add a function into a spreadsheet, learn PHP, or change your oil? It is all on YouTube. YouTube is also doing a much better job these days in both removing the pirated content, and allowing for a legitimate way to watch movies and television shows via rental or purchase. This is another way for Google (who owns YouTube) to compete with Amazon Prime, and Apple TV and, in my opinion, they have the most robust inventory of rental content. If I can't find it for free on Netflix of Amazon Prime, this is where I look next. It is also a great place to watch content from lots of television stations, like Bloomberg, for free.

Network TV Apps

Some networks let you watch their programming online or via their app without a cable subscription, but many still require you to pay a monthly service fee to a provider. Here is a breakdown of the most popular networks. If your favorite didn't make this list, you can check by going to their website.

Some terms I use:

CABLE REQUIRED means that although they might stream shows on their website or app, they won't give you access without a cable subscription.

Internet Friendly – Means that they stream lots of their popular shows from their website or app.

SLING means the channel is included with a basic Sling TV subscription.

A&E – SLING – The app uses a hybrid model where it unlocks certain episodes for cord cutters online, but requires you to log in with your cable provider or SLING for much of their content.

Adult Swim – SLING.

AMC – CABLE REQUIRED or SLING. You can also find lots of their most recent popular content, like *The Walking Dead*, on Hulu. Other shows, like *Mad Men*, are available to rent (a fee for each episode!) from subscription sites like Amazon.

ABC – Unlike CBS and NBC, ABC wants you to have a cable subscription before they let you watch all of the content on their app, WatchABC, although they make a few shows available to try to hook you. You can still get their shows live with an HDMI antenna, or, they suggest, with a HULU Plus subscription.

Like the other big three, ABC has a news app that streams print and video. They do not appear to have a separate sports app.

Bravo – Bravo uses the hybrid model where they make some shows available on their app, and some you have to have a cable subscription to unlock.

HULU carries a lot of their shows, so you can still get your *Real Housewives* action.

CBS – Internet Friendly - CBS has a free app that lets you watch network shows the day after they air, including soap operas like *The Bold and The Beautiful.* They have an additional package, CBS All Access for $5.99 per month to let you stream live shows like sports (but not CBSSports, that is a different channel), etc. You can get the same thing for free with an HDMI antenna. But with All Access, you also get past seasons and some vintage shows. They are the only big network so far to offer cord cutters a subscription. Netflix has past seasons of many of their shows if you are trying to get caught up on a new favorite.

CBS, like the other major networks, has a separate news app which has both video and print content.

CBS Sports is a different story. This is a premium channel. I recently wanted to watch a college game that was on CBS Sports, and couldn't find a way to access it without cable. I listened to it on the radio instead. This isn't a big issue for me, but it could be for someone who regularly watches games on that channel.

Comedy Central – The website and app allow viewers to access only some content without cable. HULU has a few of their shows as well.

CW – Internet Friendly - The CW lets you stream full episodes from their website or app, except they require users to disable ad blockers. Fair enough. Even better, they have another channel CWSEED that has entire seasons of a few cult classics, and new shows (short in length, 5-10 minutes each) of new shows, like the *Veronica Mars* spin-off, *Play It Again, Dick*.

Discovery Channel – App and website have recent episodes of a few of their popular shows, namely *MythBusters* and *Gold Rush*. Some shows are also on HULU.

Disney – SLING. The Disney Channel will also let you watch recent episodes of some shows on their website or app, while others they lock unless you are a cable subscriber. Movies you still need to purchase or rent.

ESPN – SLING - ESPN has an app called WATCHESPN. You need a subscription to view all of the content from all ESPN channels. As of this printing, ESPN, won't sell cord cutters a standalone subscription, but you get access for free with a $20 monthly Sling TV subscription.

Esquire – Esquire uses the model where they let you watch a few episodes for free, but for the most part you need to sign in with your cable provider for full access.

Food Network – SLING – The Food Network Doesn't seem to have a separate television show app, although I could be wrong. To stream shows live from their website, you need a cable log in. I have found great third party apps which list restaurants that have been featured on the Food Network, but that is a different story. Netflix has past seasons of popular shows like *Chopped,* and *Diners, Drive-Ins and Dives.*

FX – CABLE ONLY – Netflix has past seasons of popular shows like *American Horry Story* and *Sons of Anarchy.*

Fox- Fox has an app called FoxNow that has only select episodes available for cord cutters, including the latest episode(s) of many of their most popular shows. You need a cable subscription to watch everything on their site. Hulu seems to have lots of Fox content as well.

Fox has a FoxNews app, with video and print, just like ABC, NBC, and CBS. And like the big three, Fox Sports also has an app, which requires a cable subscription.

Hallmark Channel – CABLE ONLY.

HBO - HBO NOW is about $15 per month. HBO has two online streaming channels. HBO GO, and HBO NOW. HBO GO is only available if you pay for the channel through a cable subscription. For years, many people just borrowed someone else's login information and watched the channel "at a friend's house." HBO has traditionally turned a blind eye to this behavior and claimed that, far from damaging its bottom line, it the best advertising pipeline for its product. But in early 2015 they rolled out HBO NOW, an online-only subscription. There is a big caveat. At first, the only streaming device you could watch it on was Apple TV, although you could also watch it on a computer over the internet once you signed up via iTunes. It became a two-step process, login on your laptop and cast it to your device or connect it via an HDMI cable. Now it is also available on Chromecast, and Fire TV. No word yet about other devices like ROKU. HBO NOW is also a $15 add on channel if you sign up for a Sling TV monthly subscription, which is a way to legally get it if you have ROKU.

HGTV – CABLE ONLY + SLING. A few of their most popular shows are also on Netflix, like *Property Brothers*.

H2- Internet Friendly + SLING. Watch full episodes of recent shows online.

History Channel – Internet Friendly + SLING. The History Channel has the most recent episodes of their most popular shows online for streaming. For past seasons, though, you have to go to a rental site like Amazon and pay by the episode or season.

Lifetime – CABLE ONLY + SLING. Also, of the most popular shows like *Dance Moms* and *Project Runway* are on HULU.

MTV – Internet Friendly - Watch full episodes on their website, app or HULU.

NBC – Internet Friendly - NBC streams many of their popular shows online, like news, *Blacklist* and

Days of Our Lives. They have an app as well (not for windows yet, but you don't really need an app if you can go right to their site). Netflix has past seasons of the most popular shows if you are still trying to get caught up.

NBC has a separate news app with video and print content, like the other networks.

The NBCSports app is free, but you need a cable subscription to stream the content.

Nick Jr. – Nick Jr. will let you stream some content while it keeps certain shows locked up for cable subscribers.

Nickelodeon – Nickelodeon has a few free episodes, but the majority requires a cable subscription.

PBS – Internet Friendly - PBS will let you watch recent episodes of their popular shows on their website and apps (I didn't see one for windows yet).

Amazon Prime subscribers can get back episodes of Downton Abbey and Mr. Selfridge for free, but they need to pay for other shows.

Spike TV – CABLE ONLY, but lots of their shows are on HULU.

Showtime – Subscriptions run about $10.99 per month.

TBS – CABLE ONLY + SLING. I can't find any of their programming on HULU or Netflix.

TNT – CABLE ONLY + SLING. HULU carries a couple of shows, *The Last Ship*, and *Murder in the First*. Amazon will let you rent episodes of other programs like *The Librarians*, but it isn't cost effective if you have a lot of favorites on that channel.

USA – CABLE ONLY. HULU seems like it has their shows, but when you try to download, it says they are unavailable. Amazon is happy to rent you individual episodes of popular shows like *Mr. Robot,* but it can get pricey to watch an entire season. If you are a big fan of USA programming, cord-cutting might not be a cost effective solution for you unless you are willing to break some rules.

It is easy when you look at the above list to get caught up on what is not available currently to cord cutters. What isn't immediately apparent is all of the quality shows and movies that are available, movies, in particular, and entire television seasons that you can't see if you only have cable. This is why I suggest you add a streaming device first for a few months, and then evaluate what you are watching the most from there.

None of the channels in this chapter address the issue of live programming, in particular how cord cutters can watch live sporting events. The next chapter shows you how to get access to your favorite teams and players.

Chapter Five: Sports

Most sports are pretty easy to get, and I'll give you a link to where you can buy a subscription. There are sites that stream all kinds of sports action for free, but you need to be really, really careful. If you choose to go this route, DO NOT DOWNLOAD ANYTHING, ever. Often, these sites will tell you that you need to download certain software to watch the game, and once you do, your computer stops working properly. Most sports fans are happy to pay for a lawful subscription to watch their favorite matches. And most sports organizations are happy to oblige. Except for the NFL. They are a bit trickier, but I have high hope that within a few years they will come on board.

First let's look at the 2000-pound gorilla in the room.

NFL

If you live outside of the United States or Mexico, NFL is easy. You go to nfl.com/gamepass and for roughly $150 you can watch any game(s) (because you can split the screen) live or after the fact any time you want. If you live in the US, the agreement the NFL has with Direct TV Sunday Ticket means that you have to jump through a few hoops. Direct TV offers internet access in addition to their dish subscription, but not instead of it. Last year they rolled out online only subscriptions on an extremely limited basis to a few colleges. When I called so see if I could sign up, the representative told me I was out of luck and to "borrow a friend's login." I don't believe that is their official company policy.

This year, Direct TV has said it will increase its online-only availability, but they have no details yet on their website. AT&T now owns Direct TV, and they have hinted at Sunday Ticket being made available for mobile phone users without a dish subscription, but that is only rumor and speculation at this point.

NFL.com/gamepass has increased its offerings for US subscribers somewhat for 2015. You can now watch preseason games live, listen to the audio to any game live, and watch any game the day after it is played.

However, if you use an ad blocker, such as AdFreeTime (for about $3 a month) to mask your location, you can sign up and get the full package that subscribers out of the country enjoy. Is that legal? Probably not. But I have no doubt that the thousands of users who did it are one of the two main reasons that the NFL.com/gamepass package includes so much this year (the other reason being people who watch games 'at a friend's house'), and that users who continue to do it will force either the NFL or Direct TV to eventually suck it up and sort it out. As for me, the subscription will let me continue to enjoy watching football as I'm vacationing in sunny Costa Rica during the rainy season.

If you are only interested in watching your home team, you can catch most of the local games (provided no local blackout) and the nationally televised ones via an HD antenna on a local channel.

In 2014, all of the Sunday night games were streamed live over the internet by the NFL. In 2013, most of the other national games were streamed live as well, so that trend is headed in the wrong direction. As of this writing, I can't out find if the NFL is committed to streaming any games for the 2015 season.

MLB

Catch your local games with an HD antenna. You can get a subscription to all out of market games at MLB.TV for $24.99 per year, but they do blackout the nationally televised games. Some games also will be on ESPN if you have a Sling TV subscription.

NHL

If hockey is your thing, you can watch local games and the nationally televised ones with an HDMI antenna. You can also get it directly from the gamecenter.nhl.com with a subscription.

NBA

If the basketball team you follow is local, you might be able to watch games with nothing more than an HDMI antenna. Or if you have a Sling TV subscription, lots of games are broadcast on ESPN and TNT. You can catch select TNT games for free on http://www.nba.com/tntovertime/, and get bonuses like multiple camera angles. Alternately, you can get a subscription directly from http://www.nba.com/leaguepass/ for a single game, team, or the entire league. If you are subject to league blackouts based on your location, you can get around it by masking your location. See the chapter on hacks for more details.

College Football

If you want more NCAA action than you get on your local channels, ESPN shows over half the games. You can get access to WatchESPN through a Sling TV subscription. However, some games you can't get online, like the ones shown on CBSSports, so check your teams' websites so see where their games are broadcast before making a switch. For instance, most of CUs (Colorado University) games are shown on PAC-12 Networks, which is available only with a cable subscription right now. A few CU games are streamed live on the internet, but not enough to please a rabid fan.

Golf

The Golf Channel is owned by NBC, and as, per this writing, they are unwilling to sell a subscription to cord cutters, thereby encouraging renegades to borrow logins and passwords from their cable subscribing friends. You can get the majors using an HDMI antenna and on ESPN through Sling TV.

Cycling

NBC will sell you an online subscription to stream the Tour de France for $30, look at http://www.cutcabletoday.com/tour-de-france-live-stream/. Sling International streams other races, like the Tour Down Under, Tour of Belgium, and Tour de Suisse.

Soccer

The world's most popular sport is catching on in the US. You can get Champion's League and the Women's World Cup on Fox Soccer to Go. Fubo Pro, at $6.99 per month, shows live matches from La Liga, Serie A, MLS, Liga MX, Eredivisie, Ligue 1, Primeira Lega, Brazilian Serie A, and championships games from Copa America, Copa America Centenario, CONMEBOL, Football League Championship, English League Cup, and Super Swiss League.

Sling TV also has lots of soccer, through ESPN.

Keep in mind that many sports games are also broadcast over the radio, for free. If you like to listen while doing something else, radio might be an answer for you.

Once you figure out if sports are going to limit your conversion from cable to the internet, take a look at the next chapter on hacks to learn a few advanced technics to ramp up your cord cutting experience.

Chapter Six: Hacks

Once you start streaming, you'll realize that there is room for improvement in your digital TV watching experience. You can't fast forward through the ads, some content is blocked because of your location, and if doesn't feel very organized. Remember, this is the Wild West, where the rules are still being written, and anything goes. Some of these solutions might not be legal in your country of residence, so proceed at your own risk.

Add Your Own Digital Library into the Mix

If you already have a large library of DVDs and other forms of digital media, you can download an app like Plex to organize and share them between your devices. Full subscriptions are about $4 a month. Then, upload your media, and Plex becomes a server, sending those movies and shows to your other devices when you want to watch them.

Block Ads

Want to Block ads from YouTube, network television sites, and websites in general? All you need is a monthly subscription to a website like AdFreeTime, and to download the software. For about $2 a month, you can eliminate a lot of the annoying ads that pop up on websites, along with commercials in many television shows. It keeps your computer safer because it blocks a lot a dangerous stuff. It also blocks your location, which is a big privacy bonus, and allows you to access content from all over the world.

Block Your Location

With either a VPN (virtual private network) or a monthly subscription to an ad blocker like AdFreeTime, you can mask your location, opening up any content that has been geoblocked because of your location. Want to watch American Netflix but you can't because you like in Australia? Now you can. Want to watch Downton Abbey on BBC instead of PBS three months later? With an adblocker, you can.

Want a subscription to gamepass.NFL.com to watch all games all season (or just your home team), but you can't because you live in the US or Mexico? You can remove the restriction with an ad blocker. Using an ad blocker to access geoblocked content may not be legal in your country so make sure to check first. Since you will still be subject to subscription fees, content providers seem happy enough to turn a blind eye, so far, but that could change, so do so at your own risk.

Library

In addition to stocking DVD movies and seasons of your favorite shows, your local library probably has access to a number of video streaming subscription services, including OverDrive, and Hoopla. All you need is a free library card. The content will vary greatly depending on the library, so the more library cards you have, the better.

Popcorn Time

Want all your movies and TV shows on one channel without any commercials or fees? TV episodes as they appear in the networks, movies as soon as they disappear from theaters? No problem. Seriously. Download the Popcorntime.io app (note that this is different than Popcorn Flix), and you'll have it all. The catch? It probably isn't legal in your country. Right now, no one seems interested in hunting down and prosecuting users, but that could always change. Whether you feel it is moral is an entirely different question. With apps like Popcorn Time, you are streaming copyrighted content without paying the content creators for it. Which is why you won't find the channel on your Roku or Apple TV box. But you can get it on your computer and project it onto the bigger screen.

Most people who stream through Popcorn Time would be happy to pay monthly for the well-organized, all in one place content. This is the experience that cord cutters want, designed and executed by "Geeks from Around the World." The reason that the sanctioned cord cutting experience is so disorganized in comparison is because content providers all want to be in control instead of concentrating on the end user experience. My guess is that Popcorn Time will eventually be blocked in the United States (like it is in the UK). I'm somewhat surprised it hasn't been already. But what it has done is forced other providers to take notice, and they are starting to change the way they provide content because of it.

Is there any risk to the Popcorn Time app?

Yes, there are at least two risks to be aware of. The first is that there is no guarantee that the content you stream won't have viruses or malware attached. Because they use torrents it is less likely, and none of the users I have talked to have experienced issues, but it is possible.

Secondly, when you stream from a sit that uses torrents, you are not only receiving the content, you are also broadcasting it while you are watching it. So if the authorities want to hunt down the users, you will be easy to find, unless you are using a VPN. And even then they can probably still find you if they really want.

Private Channels:

Not all channels are listed in your Roku channel store. It may be that they are adult channels, religious channels, or unofficial content, but there is a way to add many of them if you know the secret code. Find an unofficial list at http://mkvxstream.blogspot.com/2015/04/roku-private-channels-2015-roku.html.

Saving Streamed Content

Sometimes you want to be able to download content and watch it later, perhaps on a car ride or an airplane trip. Instead of streaming from your favorite channel, can you store it for later? The answer is a very qualified, sometimes.

There are two main issues with storing streamed content. The first is that it usually violates the terms of the streaming service; the fear is that you are going to copy and distribute copyrighted content. The second problem is that if you download a 'free download helper', you are likely to get more than you bargained for in the form of malware or viruses on your hard drive. Never download anything if you don't know what it is, especially if it is free.

There are some people who are sophisticated enough to find the streamed content in their temporary internet file folder and can amalgamate the files into something useful.

Some folks use sites like www.savefrom.net to download YouTube videos (don't download their helper if you use it!). Some people buy software like Audials Moviebox to download and save streaming content. I have never tried it, but rumor has it that Audials works on Netflix and Pandora too, though they don't advertise it for obvious reasons.

If you want to stay squeaky clean, the best way is to buy the content from a site that permits downloading purchased content, like iTunes.

Website vs. App

Some networks let you stream content for free on their website but require a cable subscription for their channel or app. The opposite is true for other networks. Make sure you check both.

Using a computer instead of a streaming device

Rather than buying a separate streaming device, a laptop running windows 8 or higher will hook up to your television with an HDMI cable, and allow you the widest content variety. You can download apps, watch content from websites, and take advantage of all the different platforms.

Chapter Seven: Resources

Because the world of cord-cutting is still so new, changes happen all the time So where can you keep up to date with the biggest changes and trends?

One of the best ways I keep up with what is going on is to ask other people. When I'm getting my hair cut (and colored, shhhhhhh), I ask my hairdresser what shows he is watching these days. I listen when my friends talk about their new Apple TV. I scroll through my mother's cable channels and DVR when I stay with her. I'm not aggressive about staying up to date, but I do keep my eyes and ears open. The best place to learn about something new is from someone else who is excited about it.

I also scan the new and social media apps for new data. If you like to read blogs, here are three blogs you can look at regularly for updated information:

http://www.digitaltrends.com/topic/cord-cutting-101/

http://cordcuttersnews.com/

https://www.techdirt.com/blog/?tag=cord+cuttin
g

Resources listed in other chapters:

Please note that because of the nature of the internet,
it is possible that some of these have moved or
changed.

To find where you can watch a specific television
show or movie is: www.moreflicks.com

To test your internet speed: www.speedtest.net

To record shows you stream (make sure to keep it
legal): http://audials.com/en/start/

To block ads online: https://adfreetime.com

Amazon channels:
http://www.amazon.com/b/ref=sv_mas_4?ie=UT
F8&node=7031433011

Apple TV Channels:
http://www.apple.com/tv/entertainment/

Chromecast Channels:
https://www.google.com/intl/en_us/chromecast/apps/?utm_source=chromecast.com

Roku Channels:
https://channelstore.roku.com/browse/movies-and-tv/popularity

Roku Private Channels:

http://mkvxstream.blogspot.com/2015/04/roku-private-channels-2015-roku.html

Xbox Channels:

http://www.xbox.com/en-US/entertainment/xbox-360/live-apps

To see what movies you can stream from your library: https://www.overdrive.com/, www.hoopla.com

Sports Subscription sites:

MLB: http://mlb.mlb.com

NFL: https://gamepass.nfl.com

NBA: http://www.nba.com/leaguepass/

NHL: https://subscribe.nhl.com/

Soccer: http://www.foxsoccer2go.com, https://www.fubo.tv

A Note from the Author

Dear Reader,

For over a decade, I worked with brilliant people at regional investment banks and investment firms who were intimidated by technology. It didn't matter how smart they were. If someone didn't grow up using computers, then it was fairly easy for them to get overwhelmed when something went wrong with a computer program. This doesn't apply to everyone, of course. Some people just naturally get technology. But many other people do not.

It is different for children. They aren't afraid to push (literal and figurative) buttons. Their openness to trying the new, and their lack of fear when they do so, means that they adapt and learn easily. But older generations, who grew up living in real, rather than virtual, communities, have a different understanding of consequence. When you push a button in the real world, something happens, so you better know what it is before you push it. Older people are often more cautious. They are mindful of Newton's Second Law, and that makes them less eager to tap about and see what happens. Their wisdom and experience is their technological downfall.

Because older generations often delay before embracing new technology, they can miss out on the good that devices or programs can offer. My desire is to help bridge that gap, to help people both become aware of new technology that would make their life easier or happier and to teach them how to use it. Besides being a self-described computer nerd, I have a formal education in technology. I received a Bachelor's of Science in computer programming from Regis University in 2002, and I was also the recipient of the *Lady Ada Lovelace Award for Excellence in Computer Information or Science* the same year.

These days, I no longer work for big corporations. I homeschool my two children and travel with them and my husband as much as we can. When we are not road tripping, we live in western Colorado.

If you have a question about something you read in this book, have another topic you'd like more information about, or just want to share with me an opinion, you can reach me on twitter @TechRx4Seniors, on my Facebook page Lose Your Cable, or by email jjstreetman@brightideaseditoria.com.

If you like this book, I'd really appreciate it if you'd take a moment to leave a review on Amazon. Your comments are the best way for other readers to decide if this book should be on their shortlist.

Sincerely,

J. J. Streetman

Other Books Published by Bright Ideas Editoria Ltd.

Francesca DiMarco

The 8 Day Green Smoothie Cleanse: Lose up to 13 Pounds in 8 Days with 25 Delicious Recipes

10 Day Sugar Detox Diet: Smash Your Addiction and Cravings! Lose Weight! Includes 10 Day Meal Plan and 30 Savory Recipe

Francesca DiMarco with Kostas Magoulas

The Mediterranean Diet Cookbook for Beginners...Who Love to Eat: Lose Weight with 75 Authentic Recipes

Ryan J.S. Martin

10,000 Steps: Walking for Weight Loss, Walking for Health: A Turn by Turn Roadmap (Weight Loss Series)

Magnesium Deficiency: Weight Loss, Heart Disease and Depression, 13 Ways that Curing Your Magnesium Deficiency Can Rejuvenate Your Body

The Vitamin D Cure: 8 Surprising Ways Curing Your Undiagnosed Vitamin D Deficiency Can Revitalize Your Health, Prevent Cancer and Heart Disease, and Help You Lose Weight

[1] https://www.fcc.gov/guides/household-broadband-guide
[2] http://www.pcworld.com/article/2011293/how-to-know-when-its-time-to-replace-your-router.html